Published By Robert Corbin

@ Clarence Nixon

Carnivore Cuisine: A Beginner's Recipe

Collection

All Right RESERVED

ISBN 978-87-94477-29-1

TABLE OF CONTENTS

Chicken Caesar Wrap 1

Smoky Bbq Beef Jerky Bites 3

Spicy Teriyaki Beef Jerky Bites... 6

Breakfast Bowl 9

Breakfast Sandwich 11

Grilled Chicken And Avocado Salad................................. 13

Slow Cooked Beef Brisket With Spices............................ 15

Grilled Lamb Chops With Rosemary................................ 16

Spicy Cajun Shrimp Skewers.. 19

Ham And Cheese Omelets... 21

Steak And Avocado Breakfast Bowl: 23

Salmon And Cream Cheese Rollups 24

Lemon Chicken Roast 25

Bacon Chicken Meatballs 27

Delicious Chicken Soup 29

Ruminant Stock 31

Poultry Stock 33

Pulled Pork Omelet 35

Grilled Lamb Chops With Herbs And Vegetables 37

Smoked Salmon With Cream Cheese 38

Meatballs With Barbecue Sauce 40

Prosciuttowrapped Asparagus 42

Chicken Liver Pâté 44

Bacon And Cheese Frittata 46

Sausage And Cheese Breakfast Casserole 48

Turkey And Bacon Lettuce Wraps 51

Beef And Broccoli Skillet 54

Berry Parfait 57

Frozen Banana Pops 59

Buffalo Chicken Burgers 61

Baked Salmon With Lemon Cream Sauce: 63

Perfectly Crispy Bacon And Sunny Side Up Eggs 65

Bacon Wrapped Egg Cups 67

Baked Salmon 69

Grilled Steak 71

Crispy Skin Duck Breast With Orange Glaze 72

Grilled Tuna Steaks With Cilantro Lime Butter 74

Grilled Rib Eye Steak With Grilled Asparagus 76

Baked Salmon With Lemon Butter 78

Roasted Turkey 80

Cheesy Bacon Chicken 83

Steak And Egg Tacos 85

Grilled Chicken Breasts With A Roasted Vegetable Salad 87

Caprese Skewers With Tomatoes And Mozzarella 89

Mixed Salami Antipasto 91

Baconwrapped Shrimp 92

Carnivore Lettuce Wraps 94

Salmon Fillet With Lemon Butter 96

Smoked Salmon And Cream Cheese On A Bed Of Lettuce 98

Ham And Cheese Rollups With A Side Of Avocado 100

Chocolate Avocado Mousse 102

Coconut Chiai Pudding 104

Baked Garlic Parmesan Wings 106

Slow Cooker Barbecue Ribs 107

Bacon And Scrambled Eggs With Cheddar Cheese 109

Classic Ribn Eye Steak And Eggs Skillet 111

Baked Chicken Breasts 113

Grilled Pork Chops 114

Herb Roasted Chicken Breast With Garlic 115

Bacon Wrapped Filet Mignon With Mushroom Sauce. 116

Grilled Lamb Chops With Rosemary 119

Pork Tenderloin With Garlic Butter 120

Chicken Casserole 122

Baked Chicken Wings 124

Easy Turkey Patties 125

Sliced Steak With Steamed Broccoli And Roasted
Potatoes 127

Turkey Burgers With Sweet Potato Fries 129

Veal Chops Stuffed With Cheese And Olives 131

Chicken Salad With Walnuts And Mustard Sauce 133

Tuna Salad Stuffed Avocado 135

Beef And Broccoli Stirfry 137

Chicken Caesar Wrap

Ingredients:

- 1/4 tsp black pepper
- 4 large tortillas
- 1/2 cup Caesar dressing
- 1/2 cup shredded Parmesan cheese
- 1/4 cup diced tomatoes
- 2 boneless, skinless chicken breasts
- 2 tsp olive oil
- 1/2 tsp garlic powder
- 1/2 tsp onion powder
- 1/2 tsp dried oregano

- 1/2 tsp salt

Directions:

1. Heat a large skillet over medium high heat.
2. Rub chicken with olive oil, garlic powder, onion powder, oregano, salt and pepper.
3. Sear chicken for 34 minutes per side or until cooked through.
4. Remove chicken from the skillet and let rest for 510 minutes before slicing.
5. Slice chicken and assemble wraps by layering chicken, Parmesan cheese, tomatoes and Caesar dressing onto the tortillas.
6. Roll up the tortillas and secure with toothpicks.
7. Serve immediately and enjoy!

Smoky Bbq Beef Jerky Bites

Ingredients:

- 1 tablespoon smoked paprika

- 1 teaspoon garlic powder

- 1 teaspoon onion powder

- 1/2 teaspoon sea salt (optional, if not using tamari sauce)

- Pinch of cayenne pepper (optional, for added heat)

- 1 pound of high quality beef (e.g., sirloin or brisket), thinly sliced against the grain

- 1/4 cup coconut amines or tamari sauce

- 2 tablespoons apple cider vinegar

- 2 tablespoons tomato paste

Directions:

1. In a bowl, combine the coconut aminos or tamari sauce, apple cider vinegar, tomato paste, smoked paprika, garlic powder, onion powder, sea salt (if using), and cayenne pepper (if desired) to create the smoky BBQ marinade.
2. Add the thinly sliced beef to the marinade, ensuring each piece is thoroughly coated. Cover the bowl and refrigerate for at least 4 hours or overnight for maximum flavor infusion.
3. Preheat your oven to 175°F (80°C) or the lowest setting possible.
4. Remove the marinated beef slices from the refrigerator and pat them dry with paper towels to remove excess marinade.

5. Arrange the beef slices on a baking sheet lined with parchment paper or a wire rack placed on a baking sheet.
6. Place the baking sheet in the preheated oven and bake the beef slices for 34 hours or until they become firm and chewy, yet still moist.
7. Let the smoky BBQ beef jerky bites cool completely before storing them in an airtight container. Relish the rich and savory flavors of this smoky delight as a satisfying and nutrient dense snack.

Spicy Teriyaki Beef Jerky Bites

Ingredients:

- 1 tablespoon sesame oil

- 1 teaspoon freshly grated ginger

- 1 teaspoon garlic powder

- 1/2 teaspoon red pepper flakes (adjust to desired level of heat)

- 1/2 teaspoon sea salt (optional, if not using tamari sauce)

- 1 pound of high quality beef (e.g., ribeye or top sirloin), thinly sliced against the grain

- 1/4 cup coconut amines or tamari sauce

- 2 tablespoons apple cider vinegar

- 2 tablespoons honey (optional, for a touch of sweetness)

- 1 tablespoon toasted sesame seeds (optional, for added texture)

Directions:

1. In a bowl, combine the coconut aminos or tamari sauce, apple cider vinegar, honey (if using), sesame oil, grated ginger, garlic powder, red pepper flakes, sea salt (if using), and toasted sesame seeds (if desired) to create the spicy teriyaki marinade.

2. Add the thinly sliced beef to the marinade, ensuring all pieces are thoroughly coated. Cover the bowl and refrigerate for at least 4 hours or overnight for optimal flavor infusion.

3. Preheat your oven to 175°F (80°C) or the lowest setting possible.

4. Remove the marinated beef slices from the refrigerator and pat them dry with paper towels to remove excess marinade.
5. Arrange the beef slices on a baking sheet lined with parchment paper or a wire rack placed on a baking sheet.
6. Place the baking sheet in the preheated oven and bake the beef slices for 34 hours or until they become chewy and flavorful, with a hint of spiciness.
7. Let the spicy teriyaki beef jerky bites cool completely before storing them in an airtight container. Indulge in this zesty and protein packed snack, enjoying the perfect balance of heat and sweetness.

Breakfast Bowl

Ingredients:

- 1 diced onion

- 2 cups of spinach

- 4 eggs

- 4 slices of bacon

- 2 tablespoons of butter

- 1 diced sweet potato

- Salt and pepper to taste

Directions:

1. Inside a large pan over medium heat, fry the bacon until it is crisp. To drain, place aside on a paper towel.

2. In the same skillet, melt the butter and add the sweet potato and onion. The veggies should be cooked for around 10 minutes, stirring once or twice.
3. Add the spinach and cook for another 3 minutes.
4. Push the vegetables to the side of the skillet and crack the eggs into the empty space. Sprinkle with salt and pepper.
5. Cook until the eggs are cooked to your desired doneness.
6. Place the vegetables in a bowl and top with the bacon and eggs. Serve and enjoy.

Breakfast Sandwich

Ingredients:

- 4 eggs

- 4 slices of bread

- 4 slices of cheese

- 4 slices of bacon

- 2 tablespoons of butter

- Salt and pepper to taste

Directions:

1. Inside a large pan over medium heat, fry the bacon until it is crisp. To drain, place aside on a paper towel.

2. In the same skillet, melt the butter and crack the eggs into the skillet. Sprinkle with salt and pepper.
3. Cook until the eggs are cooked to your desired doneness.
4. Place a slice of cheese on each slice of bread and top with an egg and bacon.
5. Top with the second piece of bread and softly push down.
6. Serve and enjoy.

Grilled Chicken And Avocado Salad

Ingredients:

- 2 cups baby spinach

- 2 cups baby arugula

- 2 tablespoons crumbled feta cheese

- 2 tablespoons chopped toasted almonds

- 2 boneless, skinless chicken breasts

- 1 ripe avocado, diced

- 2 tablespoons olive oil

- 2 tablespoons freshly squeezed lemon juice

- Salt and pepper, to taste

Directions:

1. Preheat the grill to medium high heat.
2. After applying olive oil, season the chicken breasts with chilli & salt..
3. Grill the chicken until fully done, about 6 to 8 minutes each side.
4. Turn off the heat and let the food five minutes to cool.
5. In the meanwhile, mix the spinach, arugula, feta cheese, and almonds in a big bowl.
6. Combine the lemon juice and olive oil in a small bowl.
7. Slice the chicken into strips and add to the salad.
8. Drizzle the dressing over the salad and toss to combine.
9. Serve the salad with the diced avocado.

Slow Cooked Beef Brisket With Spices

Ingredients:

- 1 teaspoon onion powder

- 1 teaspoon dried oregano

- 1 teaspoon ground cumin

- 1 cup beef broth

- 2.5 lbs beef brisket

- Salt and pepper to taste

- 2 teaspoons smoked paprika

- 1 teaspoon garlic powder

Directions:

1. Preheat the oven to 325°F (165°C).

2. Season the beef brisket with salt, pepper, smoked paprika, garlic powder, onion powder, dried oregano, and ground cumin, making sure to coat both sides.
3. Place the seasoned brisket in a roasting pan or Dutch oven.
4. Pour the beef broth into the pan, making sure it reaches about 1/4 inch up the sides of the brisket.
5. Use foil or a lid to tightly cover the pan.
6. Transfer the pan to the preheated oven and cook for approximately 34 hours until the beef is fork tender.
7. Remove the brisket from the oven and let it rest for about 1015 minutes before slicing.

Grilled Lamb Chops With Rosemary

INGREDIENTS:

- 2 cloves garlic, minced

- 1 tablespoon fresh rosemary, chopped
- 4 lamb chops (approximately 1.5 lbs)
- Salt and pepper to taste
- 2 tablespoons olive oil

Directions:

1. Preheat the grill to medium high heat.
2. Add salt and pepper to both sides of the lamb chops
3. In a small bowl, mix olive oil, minced garlic, and chopped rosemary to make a marinade.
4. Brush the lamb chops with the marinade, coating them evenly.
5. Place the lamb chops on the preheated grill and cook for about 45 minutes per side for medium rare, or adjust the cooking time to your desired doneness.

6. Remove the lamb chops from the grill and let them rest for a few minutes before serving.

Spicy Cajun Shrimp Skewers

INGREDIENTS:

- 1/2 teaspoon garlic powder

- 1/2 teaspoon onion powder

- 1/4 teaspoon cayenne pepper (adjust to taste)

- Salt to taste

- Fresh parsley, chopped (for garnish)

- 2 pound of big, peeled, and deveined shrimp

- 2 tablespoons olive oil

- 1 tablespoon Cajun seasoning

- 1 teaspoon paprika

- Lemon wedges (for serving)

Directions:

1. Preheat the grill to medium high heat.
2. In a bowl, combine olive oil, Cajun seasoning, paprika, garlic powder, onion powder, cayenne pepper, and salt.
3. Add the shrimp to the bowl and toss to coat them with the spice mixture.
4. Thread the shrimp onto skewers, piercing through the tail and the head to keep them secure.
5. Grill the skewers for 2 to 3 minutes on each side, or until the shrimp are opaque and pink.
6. Take the skewers from the grill, then top them with some fresh parsley.
7. Serve with lemon wedges for squeezing over the shrimp.

Ham And Cheese Omelets

Ingredients:

- 1/4 cup shredded cheese (cheddar, Swiss, or your choice)
- Salt and pepper to taste
- Butter or cooking fat for the pan
- 4 large eggs
- 1/4 cup diced ham

Directions:

1. In a bowl, beat the eggs until well mixed.
2. Heat a nonstick skillet over medium heat and add butter or cooking fat.
3. Pour the beaten eggs into the skillet and let them cook for a minute or two until the edges start to set.

4. Sprinkle the diced ham and shredded cheese evenly over one half of the omelets.
5. Fold the other half of the omelets over the filling and press gently.
6. Cook for another minute or two until the cheese is melted and the omelets is cooked through.
7. Slide the omelets onto a plate, cut into wedges, and serve.

Steak And Avocado Breakfast Bowl:

Ingredients:

- 1 ripe avocado, sliced
- 4 large hardboiled eggs, sliced
- 1 leftover steak, sliced
- Salt and pepper to taste

Directions:

1. Arrange the sliced steak, avocado, and hardboiled eggs in a bowl.
2. Season with salt and pepper to taste.
3. Enjoy the breakfast bowl as is or drizzle with your preferred sauce or dressing (ensure it aligns with the carnivore diet).

Salmon And Cream Cheese Rollups

Ingredients:

- 46 smoked salmon slices

- 46 tablespoons cream cheese

- Optional: capers, sliced cucumber, or fresh dill for added flavor

Directions:

1. Lay the smoked salmon slices on a clean surface.
2. Spread about a tablespoon of cream cheese onto each salmon slice.
3. Add capers, sliced cucumber, or fresh dill if desired.
4. Roll up the salmon slices tightly.
5. Serve the salmon and cream cheese rollups as a protein rich breakfast option.

Lemon Chicken Roast

Ingredients:

- 1 tablespoon sea salt

- 1 lemon, zester & sliced

- 1 lemon, halved

- ½ cup ghee

- 4 lb. Whole chicken, giblets removed

Directions:

1. Start by heating your oven to 350F, and then combine your lemon zest and sea salt. Rub this into your chicken, and sprinkle the cavity with salt and stuff with lemon halves. Add in ¼ cup of ghee.

2. Brush your remaining ghee on the outside, and then put it on a roasting pan. Arrange lemon slices around your chicken.
3. Roast for one hour and fortyfive minutes.
4. Allow it to rest for ten minutes before slicing to serve. It should have reached an internal temperature of 165 before it was done.

Bacon Chicken Meatballs

Ingredients:

- 1 egg, whisked

- 1 tablespoon onion powder

- 4 tablespoons olive oil

- 2 drops liquid smoke

- 1 lb. Chicken breasts

- 8 slices chicken, cooked & crumbled

- 3 cloves garlic

- 2 sprigs parsley, fresh & torn

Directions:

1. Place all INGREDIENTS:in a food processor except for your oil or bacon grease. Pulse until well mixed.
2. Form about twenty small meatballs, and then get out a large pan for frying.
3. Heat up your oil or grease, and cook for five to ten minutes per side. Your meatballs should be done all the way through before serving.

Delicious Chicken Soup

Ingredients:

- 1/2 tsp. garlic powder

- 3 cups chicken broth

- 1 cup heavy cream

- 2 cups cheddar cheese, shredded

- 2 chicken breasts, skinless and boneless

- 2 tbsp. butter

- Pepper

- Salt

Directions:

1. Add all INGREDIENTS:except cheese and heavy cream into the instant pot and stir well.
2. Secure pot with lid and cook on high for 10 minutes.
3. Once done, release pressure using quick release then remove the lid.
4. Remove chicken from pot and shred the chicken using a fork.
5. Return shredded chicken into the pot and stir well.
6. Add cheese and cream and stir to combine.
7. Serve and enjoy.

Ruminant Stock

Ingredients:

- 3 bay leaves

- 2 sprigs fresh thyme

- 3 quarts water

- 1 tablespoon chopped fresh parsley

- 1 to 2 teaspoons salt

- 3 to 4 pounds beef or lamb shanks

- 4 to 5 carrots, coarsely chopped

- 1 small celeriac, peeled and coarsely chopped

- 1 tablespoon cider vinegar

Directions:

1. In a large pot, combine the shanks, carrots, celeriac, vinegar, bay leaves, and thyme.
2. Pour the water over all. If necessary, add additional water to cover the bones and vegetables by 1 to 2 inches. Bring to a boil; reduce the heat to low. Simmer, covered, for 5½ to 7½ hours.
3. Add the parsley and salt to the broth. Simmer, covered, for 30 minutes longer. Remove the broth from the heat and let cool.
4. Remove the bones from the broth and discard or compost. Strain the broth through a finemesh sieve into a large bowl.
5. Ladle the broth into glass jars and fasten the lids. Store in the refrigerator for up to 7 days or in the freezer for up to 1 year.

Poultry Stock

Ingredients:

- 1 tablespoon cider vinegar
- 3 bay leaves
- 2 sprigs fresh thyme
- 12 cups water
- 1 tablespoon chopped fresh parsley
- 1 whole chicken (3 to 4 pounds), cut up
- 1 small celeriac, peeled and coarsely chopped
- 4 or 5 carrots, coarsely chopped
- 1 to 2 teaspoons salt, to taste

Directions:

1. In a large pot, combine the chicken, celeriac, carrots, vinegar, bay leaves, and thyme. Pour the water over all. Bring to a boil; reduce the heat to low.
2. Simmer, covered, for 5½ to 7½ hours. Add the parsley and salt. Simmer for 30 minutes longer.
3. Remove the chicken from the stock and set aside. Strain the stock through a finemesh sieve. Let cool.
4. Remove the chicken meat from the bones. Reserve the chicken for another use or serve with some of the stock.
5. Pour the cooled stock into glass jars. Fasten the lids and store in the refrigerator for up to 7 days or in the freezer for up to 1 year.

Pulled Pork Omelet

Ingredients:

- 2 cups shredded cheese

- 8 large eggs

- 2 tablespoons olive oil

- 2 cups cooked pulled pork

- Salt and pepper to taste

Directions:

1. Heat the olive oil in a large skillet over mediumhigh heat.
2. Add the cooked pulled pork to the skillet and stir to combine.
3. In a large bowl, whisk together the eggs, salt, and pepper.

4. Pour the egg mixture into the skillet and stir to combine with the pork.
5. Allow the mixture to cook for about 5 minutes, stirring occasionally.
6. Add the shredded cheese to the skillet and stir to combine.
7. Allow the mixture to cook for an additional 5 minutes, stirring occasionally.
8. Serve the pulled pork omelet warm. Enjoy!

Grilled Lamb Chops With Herbs And Vegetables

Ingredients:

- 1 teaspoon onion powder
- 1 teaspoon dried oregano
- 1 teaspoon dried thyme
- 2 cups vegetables of your choice, diced
- 4 lamb chops
- 2 tablespoons olive oil
- 2 tablespoons fresh rosemary, chopped
- 1 teaspoon garlic powder
- Salt and pepper to taste

Directions:

1. Preheat the grill to medium high heat.
2. In a small bowl, combine the olive oil, rosemary, garlic powder, onion powder, oregano, and thyme. Mix together.
3. Rub the mixture onto the lamb chops and season with salt and pepper.
4. Place the lamb chops on the preheated grill and cook for 45 minutes per side, or until the internal temperature of the meat reaches 145 degrees Fahrenheit.
5. Add the diced vegetables to the grill and cook for 34 minutes, or until they are lightly charred and tender.
6. Serve the grilled lamb chops with the cooked vegetables. Enjoy!

Smoked Salmon With Cream Cheese

Ingredients:

- 200 g smoked salmon

- 200 g cream cheese (e.g., Philadelphia)
- Lemon juice
- Fresh herbs (such as dill or parsley)
- Salt and pepper to taste.

Directions:

1. Cut the smoked salmon into thin slices. In a bowl, mix cream cheese with lemon juice, chopped herbs, salt, and pepper to taste.
2. Make sure you get a smooth cream. Spread the cream cheese over the slices of smoked salmon. Roll the salmon slices with the cream cheese and cut them into small rolls.
3. Arrange the smoked salmon rolls with cream cheese on a serving platter.
4. Decorate with additional fresh herbs. Serve as an appetizer or finger food.

Meatballs With Barbecue Sauce

Ingredients:

- 1/4 cup finely chopped onion
- 2 cloves of garlic, finely chopped
- 2 tablespoons chopped fresh parsley
- 1/4 cup barbecue sauce
- 500 g ground beef
- 1 egg
- 1/2 cup breadcrumbs
- (plus extra for seasoning)
- Salt and pepper to taste.

Directions:

1. In a large bowl, combine ground meat, egg, bread crumbs, chopped onion, minced garlic, parsley, barbecue sauce, salt, and pepper.
2. Mix well until evenly mixed. Make meatballs of the desired size by forming small balls with your hands.
3. Preheat a nonstick skillet over medium high heat and add a drizzle of oil.
4. Place the patties in the pan and cook them for about 5 to 7 minutes on each side, until they are well browned and cooked through internally.
5. Once cooked, transfer the patties to a serving platter and season with additional barbecue sauce, if desired. Serve the meatballs with barbecue sauce as an appetizer.

Prosciuttowrapped Asparagus

Ingredients:

- 12 asparagus spears

- 6 slices of prosciutto

Directions:

1. Preheat your oven to 400°F (200°C) and line a baking sheet with parchment paper.
2. Trim the tough ends of the asparagus spears.
3. Take a slice of prosciutto and wrap it around each asparagus spear, starting from the bottom and spiraling up to the tip.
4. Place the prosciutto wrapped asparagus on the prepared baking sheet.
5. Bake in the preheated oven for 1012 minutes or until the asparagus is tender and the prosciutto is crispy.

6. Remove the Prosciutto Wrapped Asparagus from the oven and serve immediately. Enjoy this elegant and flavorful appetizer!

Chicken Liver Pâté

Ingredients:

- 1 small onion, finely chopped
- 2 garlic cloves, minced
- 2 tablespoons brandy or cognac (optional)
- 1 lb chicken livers, trimmed
- 1/2 cup butter, softened
- Salt and pepper to taste

Directions:

1. In a skillet over medium heat, melt 2 tablespoons of butter and sauté the chopped onion and minced garlic until softened.

2. Add the chicken livers to the skillet and cook until they are no longer pink inside, about 57 minutes.
3. If using brandy or cognac, add it to the skillet and cook for an additional 12 minutes to deglaze the pan.
4. Transfer the contents of the skillet to a food processor or blender.
5. Add the remaining softened butter to the food processor along with salt and pepper to taste.
6. Blend the mixture until smooth and creamy, scraping down the sides as needed.
7. Transfer the Chicken Liver Pâté to a container, cover, and refrigerate for at least 2 hours to allow the flavors to meld.
8. Serve the pâté with cucumber slices, celery sticks, or pork rinds. Enjoy this decadent and nutritious spread!

Bacon And Cheese Frittata

Ingredients:

- 1/2 cup shredded cheddar cheese
- 2 tablespoons unsalted butter
- 6 eggs
- 1/4 cup heavy cream
- 6 strips of bacon, cooked and crumbled
- Salt and black pepper to taste

Directions:

1. Preheat the oven to 375°F.
2. In a mixing bowl, whisk together the eggs and heavy cream until well combined. Season with salt and black pepper.

3. Melt the butter in a large ovensafe skillet over medium heat. Add the cooked bacon to the skillet and spread it out in an even layer.
4. Pour the egg mixture over the bacon and let cook for a minute or two, until the edges start to set.
5. Sprinkle the shredded cheese over the top of the egg mixture.
6. Transfer the skillet to the preheated oven and bake for 1012 minutes, or until the frittata is set and the cheese is melted and bubbly.
7. Remove the skillet from the oven and let cool for a few minutes before slicing and serving.
8. Enjoy your delicious Bacon and Cheese Frittata!

Sausage And Cheese Breakfast Casserole

Ingredients:

- 1 cup heavy cream
- 1 tsp garlic powder
- 1 tsp onion powder
- 1 tsp paprika
- 1/2 tsp black pepper
- 1 lb breakfast sausage
- 8 oz cream cheese, softened
- 6 large eggs
- 2 cups shredded cheddar cheese

Directions:

1. Preheat your oven to 350°F. Grease a 9x13 inch baking dish with cooking spray.
2. In a large skillet, cook the breakfast sausage over medium heat until browned and cooked through. Remove from heat and drain any excess grease.
3. In a large mixing bowl, combine the cooked sausage and softened cream cheese. Mix well until evenly combined.
4. In a separate bowl, whisk together the eggs, heavy cream, garlic powder, onion powder, paprika, and black pepper.
5. Pour the egg mixture over the sausage mixture, and stir to combine.
6. Pour the mixture into the prepared baking dish. Sprinkle the shredded cheddar cheese over the top.
7. Bake for 3540 minutes, or until the eggs are set and the cheese is melted and bubbly.

8. Let the casserole cool for a few minutes before slicing and serving.
9. Enjoy your delicious and filling Sausage and Cheese Breakfast Casserole!

Turkey And Bacon Lettuce Wraps

Ingredients:

- 1 teaspoon dried oregano
- 1 teaspoon ground cumin
- 1/2 teaspoon chili powder
- Salt and pepper to taste
- 1 head iceberg lettuce, leaves separated and washed
- 1 pound ground turkey
- 8 slices bacon, cooked and crumbled
- 1 small onion, diced
- 2 cloves garlic, minced

- Optional toppings: diced tomatoes, shredded cheese, avocado, sour cream

Directions:

1. The ground turkey should be cooked until browned in a large skillet over medium heat. As it cooks, be sure to break it up into crumbles.
2. To the skillet with the turkey, add the minced garlic and onion. The onion should soften after cooking for roughly 5 minutes.
3. Add the ground cumin, chili powder, salt, and pepper along with the dried oregano. Allow the flavors to mix together by cooking for a further two to three minutes.
4. After turning off the heat, add the bacon crumbles to the skillet. If necessary, taste and adjust the seasoning.

5. Take a lettuce leaf, and in the center of the leaf, spoon some of the turkey and bacon mixture.
6. Fold the sides of the lettuce leaf over the filling, then roll it up tightly like a burrito.
7. Repeat the process with the remaining lettuce leaves and filling until all the Ingredients: are used.
8. Serve the turkey and bacon lettuce wraps as they are, or you can garnish them with diced tomatoes, shredded cheese, avocado slices, and a dollop of sour cream.

Beef And Broccoli Skillet

Ingredients:

- 1 tablespoon cornstarch
- 2 tablespoons vegetable oil, divided
- 3 cloves garlic, minced
- 1 teaspoon grated ginger
- 1 head broccoli, cut into florets
- 1/2 cup beef broth or water
- Salt and pepper, to taste
- 1 lb (450g) beef sirloin or flank steak, thinly sliced
- 2 tablespoons soy sauce
- 2 tablespoons oyster sauce

- Optional garnish: sesame seeds, sliced green onions

Directions:

1. In a bowl, combine the soy sauce, oyster sauce, and cornstarch. Add the sliced beef and toss to coat. Let it marinate for about 1015 minutes.
2. Heat 1 tablespoon of vegetable oil in a large skillet or wok over medium high heat.
3. Add the minced garlic and grated ginger, and sauté for about 1 minute until fragrant.
4. Add the marinated beef to the skillet and stirfry for 23 minutes until it's browned on all sides. Remove the beef from the skillet and set it aside.
5. In the same skillet, add the remaining tablespoon of oil. Add the broccoli florets and stir fry for about 34 minutes until they're crisptender. If needed, you can add a splash of

water to create some steam to help cook the broccoli faster.
6. Pour the beef broth or water into the skillet with the broccoli. Cover the skillet with a lid and let it cook for another 23 minutes until the broccoli is cooked but still retains its vibrant green color.
7. Return the cooked beef to the skillet and stir everything together. Season with salt and pepper to taste.
8. Cook for an additional 12 minutes until the beef is heated through and the sauce has thickened.
9. Remove the skillet from heat. Sprinkle with sesame seeds and sliced green onions as a garnish, if desired.

Berry Parfait

Ingredients:

- 1/4 cup granola
- 1 tablespoon honey or maple syrup (optional)
- 1 cup Greek yogurt
- 1 cup mixed berries (such as strawberries, blueberries, raspberries)
- Fresh mint leaves for garnish

Directions:

1. In a glass or serving dish, layer Greek yogurt, mixed berries, and granola.
2. Repeat the layers until the Ingredients: are used, ending with a layer of berries on top.
3. Drizzle with honey or maple syrup if desired for added sweetness.

4. Garnish with fresh mint leaves.
5. Serve the berry parfait as a refreshing and nutrientpacked dessert or breakfast option.

Frozen Banana Pops

Ingredients:

- 2 ripe bananas
- 1/4 cup melted dark chocolate
- 2 tablespoons chopped nuts or shredded coconut (optional)
- Popsicle sticks or skewers

Directions:

1. Peel the bananas and cut them in half crosswise.
2. Insert a popsicle stick or skewer into each banana half, creating a handle.
3. Place the bananas on a tray lined with parchment paper and freeze for about 1 hour until firm.

4. Melt the dark chocolate in a microwave safe bowl or using a double boiler.
5. Dip each frozen banana into the melted chocolate, allowing the excess to drip off.
6. If desired, roll the chocolate coated banana in chopped nuts or shredded coconut for added texture.
7. Place the coated bananas back on the parchment lined tray and freeze for an additional 30 minutes to set.
8. Serve the frozen banana pops as a fun and healthier alternative to ice cream.

Buffalo Chicken Burgers

Ingredients:

- 1/2 tsp salt

- 1/4 tsp black pepper

- 4 hamburger buns

- 1/2 cup ranch dressing

- 1/4 cup shredded cheddar cheese

- 500g ground chicken

- 1/4 cup buffalo sauce

- 1/2 tsp garlic powder

- 1/2 tsp onion powder

- 1/2 tsp dried oregano

- 1/4 cup diced tomatoes

Directions:

1. Preheat a grill to medium high heat.
2. In a large bowl, combine ground chicken, buffalo sauce, garlic powder, onion powder, oregano, salt and pepper. Mix until well combined.
3. Form the chicken mixture into 4 patties.
4. Grill the burgers for 34 minutes per side or until cooked through.
5. Assemble burgers by layering ranch dressing, cheddar cheese, tomatoes and burgers onto the buns.
6. Serve immediately and enjoy!

Baked Salmon With Lemon Cream Sauce:

Ingredients:

- 1/2 tsp dried oregano

- 1/2 tsp salt

- 1/4 tsp black pepper

- 1/2 cup heavy cream

- 1/4 cup grated Parmesan cheese

- 1/4 cup lemon juice

- 500g salmon fillet

- 2 tsp olive oil

- 1/2 tsp garlic powder

- 1/2 tsp onion powder

- 2 tbsp butter

Directions:

1. Preheat oven to 350°F. Line a baking sheet with foil.
2. Rub salmon with olive oil, garlic powder, onion powder, oregano, salt and pepper.
3. Place salmon onto the baking sheet and bake for 1520 minutes or until cooked through.
4. Meanwhile, in a small saucepan over medium heat, combine cream, Parmesan cheese, lemon juice and butter. Simmer until sauce is thick and creamy.
5. Serve salmon with lemon cream sauce and enjoy!

Perfectly Crispy Bacon And Sunny Side Up Eggs

Ingredients:

- Thick cut bacon strips

- Fresh eggs (as many as desired)

Directions:

1. Preheat the oven to 400°F (200°C).
2. Arrange the bacon strips on a baking sheet lined with parchment paper or a wire rack placed on a baking sheet to allow the excess fat to drip off.
3. Bake the bacon in the preheated oven for 1520 minutes or until it reaches your desired level of crispiness.
4. While the bacon is cooking, heat a nonstick skillet over medium heat.
5. Crack the eggs into the skillet, being careful not to break the yolks.

6. Cook the eggs until the whites are set, and the yolks are still runny (sunnysideup). Alternatively, cook them to your preferred doneness, such as overeasy or overmedium.
7. Serve the perfectly crispy bacon alongside the sunnysideup eggs for a classic and satisfying breakfast.

Bacon Wrapped Egg Cups

Ingredients:

- Thick cut bacon strips

- Fresh eggs (as many as desired)

- Salt and pepper to taste

- Fresh chives or parsley (optional, for garnish)

Directions:

1. Preheat the oven to 375°F (190°C).
2. Grease a muffin tin or line each cup with a strip of bacon, forming a ring around the edges.
3. Crack an egg into each bacon lined cup, being careful not to break the yolk.
4. Season the eggs with salt and pepper to taste.
5. Bake in the preheated oven for 1215 minutes or until the bacon is crispy, and the eggs are cooked to your preferred doneness.

6. Remove the bacon wrapped egg cups from the muffin tin, garnish with fresh chives or parsley if desired, and serve warm.

Baked Salmon

Ingredients:

- 2 tablespoons butter
- 1 lemon, cut into wedges
- 4 (6ounce) salmon fillets
- Salt and freshly ground black pepper

Directions:

1. Preheat oven to 400 degrees F.
2. Place salmon fillets on a baking sheet lined with foil. Season with salt and pepper.
3. Place butter on top of the salmon and rub to coat the fish.
4. Bake in preheated oven for 15 minutes or until salmon is cooked through and flakes easily with a fork.

5. Serve with lemon wedges.

Grilled Steak

Ingredients:

- 2 (8ounce) steaks

- Salt and freshly ground black pepper

- 1 tablespoon olive oil

Directions:

1. Preheat grill to high heat.
2. Rub steaks with olive oil and season with salt and pepper.
3. Grill steaks for 4 minutes per side or until cooked to desired doneness.
4. Give the steaks five minutes to cool before serving.

Crispy Skin Duck Breast With Orange Glaze

Ingredients:

- 2 tablespoons honey (optional, omit for strict carnivores
- 1 teaspoon grated orange zest
- 1/2 teaspoon dried thyme
- 2 duck breasts
- Salt and pepper to taste
- 1 tablespoon olive oil
- 1/4 cup orange juice
- Fresh thyme leaves (for garnish)

Directions:

1. Place the duck breasts, skin side down, in the hot skillet and cook for about 5 minutes until the skin is crispy and golden brown.
2. Flip the duck breasts and sear for an additional 12 minutes on the other side.
3. Transfer the skillet to the preheated oven and roast the duck breasts for 810 minutes medium rare or until they reach an internal temperature of 130135°F (5457°C).
4. Remove the duck breasts from the skillet and let them rest on a cutting board, covered loosely with foil.
5. In a small saucepan, combine orange juice, honey (if using), grated orange zest, and dried thyme. Bring to a simmer over medium heat and cook until the sauce has reduced and thickened slightly.
6. Slice the duck breasts diagonally and drizzle with the orange glaze.

7. Garnish with fresh thyme leaves before serving.

Grilled Tuna Steaks With Cilantro Lime Butter

INGREDIENTS:

- 2 tablespoons unsalted butter, softened
- 2 tablespoons fresh cilantro, chopped
- 1 tablespoon lime juice
- 1 teaspoon lime zest
- 2 tuna steaks (68 oz each)
- Salt and pepper to taste
- 1/2 teaspoon minced garlic

Directions:

1. Preheat the grill to high heat.

2. On both sides, season the tuna steaks with salt and pepper.
3. In a small bowl, mix softened butter, chopped cilantro, lime juice, lime zest, and minced garlic to make the cilantro lime butter.
4. Grill the tuna steaks for about 23 minutes per side for medium rare or until desired doneness.
5. Remove the tuna steaks from the grill and let them rest for a few minutes.
6. Top the steaks with a dollop of cilantro lime butter before serving.

Grilled Rib Eye Steak With Grilled Asparagus

Ingredients:

- 2 rib eye steaks
- Asparagus spears
- Salt and pepper to taste
- Olive oil

Directions:

1. Preheat a grill to high heat.
2. Rub the ribeye steaks with olive oil and season with salt and pepper.
3. Grill the steaks to your desired level of doneness.
4. Toss the asparagus spears in olive oil, salt, and pepper.

5. Grill the asparagus for a few minutes until tender crisp.
6. Serve the grilled rib eye steaks with the grilled asparagus.

Baked Salmon With Lemon Butter

Ingredients:

- 2 tablespoons of butter

- Lemon wedges for serving

- 2 salmon fillets

- Salt and pepper to taste

Directions:

1. Preheat the oven to 400°F (200°C).
2. Season the salmon fillets with salt and pepper.
3. Place the salmon fillets on a baking sheet lined with parchment paper.
4. Top each fillet with a tablespoon of butter.

5. Bake the salmon in the preheated oven for about 1215 minutes, or until cooked to your desired doneness.
6. Serve the baked salmon with lemon wedges.

Roasted Turkey

Ingredients:

- 2 teaspoon lemon zest, grated
- 1 teaspoon fresh thyme leaves, chopped
- 1 (10pound) whole turkey, giblets removed
- 1 head garlic, cut into half crosswise
- 1 large bunch fresh thyme
- 1 Spanish onion, cut into quarters
- ¼ pound unsalted butter, melted
- 23 tablespoons fresh lemon juice
- Salt
- ¼ teaspoon freshly ground black pepper

- 1 whole lemon, halved

Directions:

1. Start by preheating your oven to 350°F.
2. In a bowl, add the butter, lemon juice, lemon zest and thyme leaves and mix well. Set aside.
3. Season the turkey cavity inside with salt and black pepper generously.
4. Arrange the turkey into a large roasting pan.
5. Fill the cavity with onion, garlic, thyme and lemon haves.
6. Rub the butter mixture on the outside of the turkey and season with black pepper and salt.
7. With kitchen string, tie the legs together and insert the tips of the wings under the turkey's body.
8. Roast for about 2½ hours.
9. Remove from the oven and palace the turkey onto a platter.

10. With a piece of foil, cover the turkey for about 1520 minutes before carving.
11. With a sharp knife, cut the turkey into desired sized pieces and serve.

Cheesy Bacon Chicken

Ingredients:

- 1/4 cup bacon, chopped
- 4 oz. cream cheese, cubed
- 2 lb. chicken breasts, skinless and boneless
- 1 cup chicken broth

Directions:

1. Set the instant pot on sauté mode.
2. Add bacon into the pot and sauté for 34 minutes.
3. Add remaining Ingredients: into the instant pot and stir well.
4. Secure pot with lid and cook on high for 12 minutes.

5. Once done, release pressure using quickrelease then remove the lid.
6. Shred the chicken using a fork and stir well.
7. Serve and enjoy.

Steak And Egg Tacos

Ingredients:

- 2 tablespoons olive oil

- Salt and pepper, to taste

- 8 small taco shells

- 4 steaks (your choice)

- 8 eggs

- 1/2 onion, diced

- 2 cloves garlic, minced

- 2 tablespoons butter

Directions:

1. Heat the olive oil in a large skillet over medium high heat.

2. Add the steaks to the skillet and season with salt and pepper. Cook the steaks until they reach desired doneness.
3. Remove the steaks from the skillet and set aside.
4. In the same skillet, add the onions and garlic. Cook until the onions are soft, about 5 minutes.
5. Push the onion and garlic to one side of the skillet and add the eggs. Scramble the eggs until they are cooked through.
6. Place the cooked steaks, eggs, and onion mixture into the taco shells.
7. Add the butter to the skillet and melt.
8. Spoon the melted butter over the tacos.
9. Serve the tacos immediately. Enjoy!

Grilled Chicken Breasts With A Roasted Vegetable Salad

Ingredients:

- 1 yellow bell pepper, cut into 1/2inch slices

- 2 tablespoons balsamic vinegar

- 2 tablespoons olive oil

- 1/2 teaspoon sugar

- 2 tablespoons chopped fresh herbs (such as oregano, basil, or thyme)

- 4 chicken breasts, skinless and boneless

- 2 tablespoons olive oil

- Salt and pepper

- 2 zucchinis, cut into 1/2inch slices

- 1 red bell pepper, cut into 1/2inch slices

Directions:

1. Preheat your grill to medium high heat.
2. Brush the chicken breasts with 2 tablespoons of olive oil, and season with salt and pepper. Grill the chicken for 45 minutes per side, or until cooked through.
3. Place the zucchini and bell pepper slices on the grill. Grill for 23 minutes per side, or until lightly charred.
4. In a small bowl, whisk together the balsamic vinegar, 2 tablespoons of olive oil, sugar, and herbs.
5. In a large bowl, combine the grilled vegetables and chicken with the dressing. Toss to combine. Serve the salad warm or cold.

Caprese Skewers With Tomatoes And Mozzarella

Ingredients:

- 200 g cherry tomatoes

- Fresh basil leaves

- Olive oil

- 200 g buffalo mozzarella cheese

- Salt and pepper to taste

- Skewers or toothpicks

Directions:

1. Cut the buffalo mozzarella into cubes or balls. Wash and dry the cherry tomatoes.
2. Take a skewer or toothpick and insert a cherry tomato, then a mozzarella cube or sphere,

and a basil leaf. Repeat until you run out of Ingredients:.
3. Arrange the Capers skewers on a serving platter. Season the skewers with a drizzle of olive oil, salt, and pepper. Serve the Capers Skewers as an appetizer.

Mixed Salami Antipasto

Ingredients:

- 100 g salami

- 100 g of prosciutto

- 100 g coppa or other cured meat of your choice, Mixed olives

- Hot peppers in oil (optional)

Directions:

1. Cut the salami, prosciutto, and copper into thin slices. Arrange the slices of cured meats on a serving platter.
2. Add mixed olives and, if desired, chilies in oil to accompany the cold cuts. Serve the mixed charcuterie appetizer with fresh bread or breadsticks.

Baconwrapped Shrimp

Ingredients:

- 12 large shrimp, peeled and deveined
- 6 slices of bacon, cut in half
- Toothpicks

Directions:

1. Preheat your oven to 400°F (200°C) and line a baking sheet with parchment paper.
2. Take a half slice of bacon and wrap it around each shrimp, securing it with a toothpick.
3. Place the bacon wrapped shrimp on the prepared baking sheet.
4. Bake in the preheated oven for 1012 minutes or until the shrimp are pink and opaque and the bacon is crispy.

5. Remove the Bacon Wrapped Shrimp from the oven and serve immediately. Enjoy these savory and satisfying appetizers!

Carnivore Lettuce Wraps

Ingredients:

- 1 tablespoon olive oil

- 2 tablespoons soy sauce (or coconut aminos for a glutenfree option)

- 2 teaspoons garlic powder

- 2 teaspoons onion powder

- 1 lb ground beef (or any other ground meat of your choice)

- Salt and pepper to taste

- Iceberg lettuce leaves (or any other large lettuce leaves)

Directions:

1. In a skillet over medium heat, heat the olive oil and brown the ground beef.
2. Season the ground beef with soy sauce, garlic powder, onion powder, salt, and pepper. Stir to combine.
3. Continue cooking the seasoned beef until it's fully cooked and nicely browned.
4. Spoon the cooked ground beef onto individual lettuce leaves to create lettuce wraps.
5. Serve your Carnivore Lettuce Wraps with additional toppings like diced tomatoes, avocado slices, or shredded cheese, if desired. Enjoy these flavorful and lowcarb wraps!

Salmon Fillet With Lemon Butter

Ingredients:

- 2 tablespoons butter, melted

- 1 lemon, juiced and zested

- 2 salmon fillets

- Salt and pepper to taste

- Fresh parsley, chopped (optional)

Directions:

1. Preheat your oven to 400°F (200°C) and line a baking sheet with parchment paper.
2. Place the salmon fillets on the prepared baking sheet.
3. In a small bowl, mix the melted butter, lemon juice, and lemon zest.

4. Brush the lemon butter mixture over the salmon fillets, coating them evenly.
5. Season the salmon with salt and pepper.
6. Bake the salmon in the preheated oven for 12-15 minutes or until it flakes easily with a fork.
7. Garnish with chopped fresh parsley, if desired. Serve your Salmon Fillet with Lemon Butter hot and enjoy the tender and tangy goodness!

Smoked Salmon And Cream Cheese On A Bed Of Lettuce

Ingredients:

- 8 oz cream cheese
- 1 head of lettuce
- 8 oz smoked salmon
- Salt and pepper to taste

Directions:

1. Rinse and dry the lettuce leaves and place them on a serving platter.
2. In a mixing bowl, combine the cream cheese with salt and pepper to taste.
3. Spread a generous layer of the cream cheese mixture on top of each lettuce leaf.

4. Cut the smoked salmon into small pieces and place them on top of the cream cheese mixture.
5. Serve immediately and enjoy!

Ham And Cheese Rollups With A Side Of Avocado

Ingredients:

- 45 slices of cheese (cheddar or Swiss)
- 1 avocado, sliced
- 810 thin slices of ham
- Salt and pepper to taste

Directions:

1. Preheat the oven to 350°F (180°C).
2. Lay the slices of ham on a flat surface, slightly overlapping each other.
3. Place the cheese slices on top of the ham.
4. Carefully roll up the ham and cheese tightly, forming a roll.
5. Place the ham and cheese rolls on a baking sheet, seam side down.

6. Bake in the oven for 10-15 minutes or until the cheese is melted and the ham is slightly crispy.
7. While the rolls are baking, slice the avocado and season with salt and pepper.
8. Serve the ham and cheese rollups with the sliced avocado on the side. Enjoy!

Chocolate Avocado Mousse

Ingredients:

- 1/4 cup honey or maple syrup
- 1/4 cup almond milk or coconut milk
- 1 teaspoon vanilla extract
- 2 ripe avocados
- 1/4 cup unsweetened cocoa powder
- Pinch of salt
- Optional toppings: whipped cream, shaved chocolate, berries

Directions:

1. In a blender or food processor, combine the ripe avocados, cocoa powder, honey or maple

syrup, almond milk or coconut milk, vanilla extract, and salt.
2. Blend until smooth and creamy, scraping down the sides as needed.
3. Taste and adjust the sweetness if desired.
4. Transfer the chocolate avocado mousse to serving dishes or glasses.
5. Chill in the refrigerator for at least 30 minutes to allow the mousse to set.
6. Before serving, add optional toppings such as whipped cream, shaved chocolate, or berries.
7. Enjoy the creamy and indulgent chocolate avocado mousse.

Coconut Chiai Pudding

Ingredients:

- 1 cup coconut milk
- 1 tablespoon honey or maple syrup
- 1/2 teaspoon vanilla extract
- 1/4 cup chia seeds
- Optional toppings: fresh fruits, shredded coconut, nuts, or seeds

Directions:

1. In a bowl, whisk together the chia seeds, coconut milk, honey or maple syrup, and vanilla extract.
2. Let the mixture sit for 5 minutes, then whisk again to break up any clumps of chia seeds.

3. Cover the bowl and refrigerate for at least 2 hours or overnight, allowing the chia seeds to absorb the liquid and form a pudding like consistency.
4. Stir the chia pudding before serving and adjust the sweetness if desired.
5. Divide the pudding into serving bowls or glasses.
6. Top with fresh fruits, shredded coconut, nuts, or seeds for added texture and flavor.
7. Enjoy the creamy and nutritious coconut chia pudding as a satisfying dessert or breakfast treat.

Baked Garlic Parmesan Wings

Ingredients:

- 1/2 tsp onion powder

- 1/2 tsp dried oregano

- 1/2 tsp salt

- 1/4 tsp black pepper

- 1/4 cup grated Parmesan cheese

- 1kg chicken wings

- 2 tsp olive oil

- 1/2 tsp garlic powder

- 2 cloves garlic, minced

Directions:

1. Preheat oven to 375°F. Line a baking sheet with foil.
2. Rub chicken wings with olive oil, garlic powder, onion powder, oregano, salt and pepper.
3. Place wings onto the baking sheet and bake for 3035 minutes or until cooked through.
4. In a small bowl, combine Parmesan cheese and garlic.
5. Remove wings from the oven and top with Parmesan cheese mixture.
6. Return wings to the oven and bake for an additional 5 minutes or until cheese is melted and bubbly.
7. Serve wings and enjoy!

Slow Cooker Barbecue Ribs

Ingredients:

- 1/2 tsp onion powder

- 1/2 tsp dried oregano

- 1/2 tsp salt

- 500g pork ribs

- 1/2 cup barbecue sauce

- 1/2 tsp garlic powder

- 1/4 tsp black pepper

Directions:

1. Place ribs into the slow cooker.
2. In a small bowl, combine barbecue sauce, garlic powder, onion powder, oregano, salt and pepper. Mix until well combined.
3. Pour the barbecue sauce mixture over the ribs.
4. Cover and cook on low for 68 hours or until ribs are tender.
5. Serve ribs with your favorite sides and enjoy!

Bacon And Scrambled Eggs With Cheddar Cheese

Ingredients:

- Thick cut bacon strips

- Fresh eggs (as many as desired)

- Cheddar cheese (shredded)

- Salt and pepper to taste

- Fresh chives or green onions (optional, for garnish)

Directions:

1. In a skillet over medium heat, cook the bacon until crispy. Remove from the skillet and drain on a paper towel.
2. In the same skillet with the bacon fat, crack the eggs and scramble them until they reach your preferred level of doneness.

3. Season the scrambled eggs with salt and pepper to taste.
4. Sprinkle shredded cheddar cheese over the scrambled eggs and allow it to melt slightly.
5. Serve the cheesy scrambled eggs alongside the crispy bacon, garnish with fresh chives or green onions if desired, and enjoy this hearty and flavorful breakfast.

Classic Ribn Eye Steak And Eggs Skillet

Ingredients:

- Rib eye steak(s), preferably grass-fed and thick cut
- Farm fresh eggs (as many as desired)
- Salt and pepper to taste
- Butter or ghee for cooking

Directions:

1. Preheat a cast iron skillet over medium high heat. Season the rib eye steak(s) generously with salt and pepper on both sides.
2. Add butter or ghee to the skillet and let it melt, creating a sizzling surface for the steak.
3. Place the rib eye steak(s) in the skillet and sear for 34 minutes on each side or until it

reaches your preferred level of doneness (medium rare is recommended for optimal tenderness and flavor).
4. Remove the cooked steak(s) from the skillet and set them aside to rest.
5. In the same skillet, crack the farm fresh eggs and cook them to your desired level of doneness, such as sunny side up, over easy, or over medium.
6. Season the eggs with a pinch of salt and pepper.
7. Arrange the cooked steak(s) and eggs in the skillet and serve immediately, savoring the succulent meat and luscious egg yolks for a hearty and satisfying breakfast.

Baked Chicken Breasts

Ingredients:

- 2 tablespoons olive oil

- 2 tablespoons fresh lemon juice

- 4 (6ounce) boneless, skinless chicken breasts

- Salt and freshly ground black pepper

Directions:

1. Preheat oven to 400 degrees F.
2. Arrange chicken breasts on a foil lined baking sheet. Season with salt and pepper.
3. Drizzle olive oil and lemon juice over the chicken.
4. Bake in preheated oven for 25 minutes or until chicken is cooked through.

5. Give the chicken five minutes to cool before serving.

Grilled Pork Chops

Ingredients:

- 4 (6ounce) pork chops
- Salt and freshly ground black pepper
- 2 tablespoons olive oil

Directions:

1. Preheat grill to high heat.
2. Rub pork chops with olive oil and season with salt and pepper.
3. Grill pork chops for 4 minutes per side or until cooked through.
4. Let the pork chops five minutes to cool before serving.

Herb Roasted Chicken Breast With Garlic

Ingredients:

- 1 teaspoon dried thyme
- 1 teaspoon dried rosemary
- 1 teaspoon dried sage
- 3 cloves garlic, minced
- 2 chicken breasts (6 oz each)
- Salt and pepper to taste
- 1 tablespoon olive oil

Directions:

1. Preheat the oven to 400°F (200°C).
2. On both sides, season the chicken breasts with salt and pepper.

3. Heat olive oil in an oven safe skillet over medium high heat.
4. Sear the chicken breasts for about 34 minutes per side until they are golden brown.
5. In a small bowl, mix dried thyme, dried rosemary, dried sage, and minced garlic to make an herb garlic mixture.
6. Sprinkle the herb garlic mixture over the seared chicken breasts, coating them evenly.
7. Transfer the skillet to the preheated oven and roast the chicken breasts for 1820 minutes until they reach an internal temperature of 165°F (74°C).
8. Remove the chicken breasts from the skillet and let them rest for a few minutes before slicing.

Bacon Wrapped Filet Mignon With Mushroom Sauce

Ingredients:

- 8 oz mushrooms, sliced
- 2 cloves garlic, minced
- 1/2 cup beef broth
- 1/4 cup heavy cream
- 2 filet mignon steaks, each weighing 6 ounces
- Salt and pepper to taste
- 4 slices of bacon
- 2 tablespoons unsalted butter
- Fresh parsley, chopped (for garnish)

Directions:

1. Preheat the oven to 400°F (200°C).
2. Season the filet mignon steaks with salt and pepper on both sides.

3. Wrap each steak with two slices of bacon, securing them with toothpicks if needed.
4. Heat a skillet over medium high heat and sear the bacon wrapped steaks for about 2 minutes on each side until the bacon is crispy.
5. Transfer the steaks to a baking dish and roast them in the preheated oven for about 810 minutes for medium rare or until desired doneness.
6. In the same skillet, melt butter over medium heat.
7. Add sliced mushrooms and minced garlic to the skillet and cook until the mushrooms are browned and tender.
8. Pour in beef broth and simmer for a few minutes until the liquid is reduced.
9. Stir in heavy cream and cook for an additional 23 minutes until the sauce thickens slightly.
10. Remove the toothpicks from the steaks and serve them with the mushroom sauce.

11. Garnish with chopped parsley before serving.

Grilled Lamb Chops With Rosemary

Ingredients:

- Lamb chops
- Fresh rosemary sprigs
- Salt and pepper to taste

Directions:

1. Preheat a grill to medium high heat.
2. Season the lamb chops with salt and pepper.
3. Place fresh rosemary sprigs on the lamb chops.
4. Grill the lamb chops for about 34 minutes per side for medium rare or adjust cooking time to your desired doneness.
5. Remove from the grill and let them rest for a few minutes before serving.

Pork Tenderloin With Garlic Butter

Ingredients:

- Pork tenderloin
- Salt and pepper to taste
- Butter
- Minced garlic

Directions:

1. Preheat the oven to 400°F (200°C).
2. Season the pork tenderloin with salt and pepper.
3. In a skillet, melt butter over medium heat and add minced garlic.
4. Sear the pork tenderloin in the skillet until browned on all sides.

5. Transfer the pork tenderloin to a baking dish and roast in the preheated oven for about 2025 minutes or until cooked through.
6. Remove from the oven and let it rest for a few minutes before slicing and serving.

Chicken Casserole

Ingredients:

- 6 oz. ham, cut into small pieces
- 5 oz. Swiss cheese
- 1 tbsp. Dijon mustard
- 2 lb. cooked chicken, shredded
- 6 oz. cream cheese, softened
- 4 oz. butter, melted
- 1/2 tsp. salt

Directions:

1. Preheat the oven to 350 F.
2. Arrange chicken in the baking dish then layer ham pieces on top.

3. Add butter, mustard, cream cheese, and salt into the blender and blend until a thick sauce.
4. Spread sauce over top of chicken and ham mixture in the baking dish.
5. Arrange Swiss cheese slices on top of sauce. Bake for 40 minutes.
6. Serve and enjoy.

Baked Chicken Wings

Ingredients:

- 1/8 tsp. paprika

- 2 tsp. seasoned salt

- 2 lb. chicken wings

- 1/4 tsp. garlic powder

Directions:

1. Preheat the oven to 400 F.
2. In a mixing bowl, add all Ingredients: except chicken wings and mix well.
3. Add chicken wings to the bowl mixture and coat well and place on a baking tray.
4. Bake 60 minutes or till cooked through.
5. Serve and enjoy.

Easy Turkey Patties

Ingredients:

- 1 garlic clove, chopped

- 1 egg, lightly beaten

- 8 oz. ground turkey

- Pepper

- Salt

Directions:

1. Add all Ingredients: into the mixing bowl and mix until well combined.
2. Make two large patties from the mixture.
3. Spray pan with cooking spray and heat over medium heat.
4. Place patties on the hot pan and cook for 45 minutes on each side.

5. Serve and enjoy.

Sliced Steak With Steamed Broccoli And Roasted Potatoes

Ingredients:

- Steak
- Broccoli
- Potatoes
- Olive oil
- Salt
- Pepper
- Garlic powder

Directions:

1. Preheat the oven to 375°F.
2. Slice the steak into thin strips.

3. Place the steak in a shallow dish and season with olive oil and salt, pepper, and garlic powder to taste.
4. Place the steak on a baking sheet and bake in the preheated oven for 10-12 minutes until cooked through.
5. Meanwhile, prepare the potatoes by cutting them into cubes and tossing with olive oil, salt, and pepper.
6. Place the potatoes on a separate baking sheet and roast in the preheated oven for 20-25 minutes until golden brown and crispy.
7. Bring a pot of water to a boil.
8. Add the broccoli to the boiling water and cook for 3-4 minutes until tender.
9. Drain the broccoli and serve with the steak and potatoes.

Turkey Burgers With Sweet Potato Fries

Ingredients:

- Onion powder

- Garlic powder

- Sweet Potatoes

- Ground Turkey

- Olive Oil

- Salt and Pepper

- Vegetable oil

Directions:

1. Preheat oven to 425 degrees F.
2. Peel and cut sweet potatoes into even sized fries. Toss with vegetable oil and spread on a

baking sheet. Bake for 2530 minutes, flipping halfway.
3. In a bowl, combine ground turkey, olive oil, salt, pepper, onion powder, and garlic powder. Mix together until everything is incorporated.
4. Form turkey mixture into patties and place on a lightly greased skillet over medium high heat.
5. Cook for 45 minutes per side, or until burgers are cooked through.
6. Serve burgers with sweet potato fries on the side. Enjoy!

Veal Chops Stuffed With Cheese And Olives

Ingredients:

- 4 thin veal chops
- String cheese cut into thin slices
- Pitted green olives, chopped
- Breadcrumbs
- Eggs, beaten
- Flour
- Salt and pepper to taste
- Olive oil for cooking

Directions:

1. Prepare thin veal chops and season them with salt and pepper on both sides.
2. Spread a slice of cheese and some chopped olives on the veal chops.
3. Roll the stuffed chops on themselves and secure them with a toothpick to keep them closed.
4. Prepare three plates: one with flour, one with beaten eggs, and one with breadcrumbs.
5. Dip the stuffed chops in the flour, then in the beaten egg, and finally in the breadcrumbs, making sure to cover each piece well.
6. Heat some olive oil in a nonstick skillet over medium high heat.
7. Add the stuffed chops to the pan and cook them for about 10 to 12 minutes per side, until they are golden brown and cooked through. Once cooked, transfer the stuffed chops to a serving platter and serve hot.

Chicken Salad With Walnuts And Mustard Sauce

Ngredients:

- 1/2 cup diced celery

- 1/2 cup raisins

- 1/4 cup mayonnaise

- 2 tablespoons mustard

- 1 tablespoon lemon juice

- 2 skinless chicken breasts

- 4 cups mixed lettuce

- 1 cup chopped walnuts

- Salt and pepper to taste.

Directions:

1. Preheat the oven to 180°C (350°F). Brush the chicken breasts with a little olive oil and season with salt and pepper.
2. Cook the chicken breasts in the preheated oven for 15 to 20 minutes, or until well done. Once cooked, let them cool for a few minutes.
3. Meanwhile, prepare the mustard sauce. In a bowl, mix the mayonnaise, mustard, lemon juice, salt, and pepper.
4. Cut the cooked chicken into cubes. In a large bowl, combine the lettuce, chopped walnuts, diced celery, raisins, and diced chicken.
5. Pour the mustard dressing over the mixture and mix well to evenly distribute the dressing.
6. Taste the salad and adjust the salt and pepper, if necessary. Serve chicken salad with walnuts and mustard sauce as a light appetizer.

Tuna Salad Stuffed Avocado

Ingredients:

- 2 tablespoons mayonnaise
- 1 celery stalk, finely chopped
- 1 tablespoon fresh lemon juice
- 2 ripe avocados, halved and pitted
- 1 can tuna, drained
- Salt and pepper to taste

Directions:

1. In a bowl, mix the drained tuna, mayonnaise, chopped celery, and fresh lemon juice.
2. Season the tuna salad with salt and pepper to taste.

3. Scoop out a bit of flesh from each avocado half to create a larger cavity for the filling.
4. Fill each avocado half with the tuna salad.
5. Serve your Tuna Salad Stuffed Avocado as a refreshing and satisfying lunch or light dinner option!

Beef And Broccoli Stirfry

Ingredients:

- 2 tablespoons coconut oil (or any cooking oil of your choice)

- 2 tablespoons soy sauce (or coconut amines for a gluten free option)

- 1 tablespoon minced garlic

- 1 lb beef sirloin or flank steak, thinly sliced

- 2 cups broccoli florets

- Salt and pepper to taste

Directions:

1. In a skillet or wok over medium high heat, heat the coconut oil.

2. Add the sliced beef to the hot oil and cook it until it's browned and cooked through.
3. Stir in the minced garlic and cook for another minute until fragrant.
4. Add the broccoli florets to the skillet and sauté them with the beef until they are tender crisp.
5. Pour the soy sauce over the beef and broccoli, tossing to coat everything evenly.
6. Season with salt and pepper to taste.
7. Serve your Beef and Broccoli Stir Fry hot and enjoy the quick and flavorful dish!